Crystal Wisdom

Crystal Wisdom

Crystal Healing, Meditation, Wisdom
and Guidance from our Angels—
What's all the fuss about?

SARAH CALDWELL

BALBOA
PRESS

A DIVISION OF HAY HOUSE

Balboa Press books may be ordered through booksellers or by contacting:

Balboa Press
A Division of Hay House
1663 Liberty Drive
Bloomington, IN 47403
www.balboapress.com.au
1-(877) 407-4847

ISBN: 978-1-4525-0275-5 (sc)
ISBN: 978-1-4525-0276-2 (e)

Printed in the United States of America

Balboa Press rev. date: 10/25/2011

Dedication:

To my children, family and friends
• without whom I would not be who I am today

Epigraph

Life is like a box of chocolates
- full of wonderful surprises

Table of Contents

List of illustrations

Preface

Crystal Wisdom—
Healing, Meditation, Wisdom and Guidance
from our Angels and Spirit Guides

What's all the fuss about?

I have written this book to share with others what I have learnt in my journey, from quiet little Catholic nerd to a full blown hippie who uses crystals, meditations, angels and spirit guides to help me live an authentic and meaningful life of health, happiness, love, peace, joy, compassion and abundance. Not that I am saying my life has been easy, or is perfect, but because of my journey and what I have learnt over the last few years in particular I am happy with where I am. Although I don't know what the future holds, for the first time I feel happy and positive about the future. I have tried to achieve this with and without my crystals and my angels and the results speak for themselves. My life is so much fuller and richer when I use and acknowledge the gifts the universe has provided me with. I want to share what I have learnt with as many people as I can—how easy it can be to change life for the better.

Not that I am a sceptic but I am generally not all that trusting either, even when things seemed to be going right I doubted the truth in my intuition, the truth of how my life changed for the better. So I spent a lot of time researching—talking to people who worked with crystals and angels cards, reading many different books, practised using meditations, crystals, angle cards and talking to my angels and guides, and tried many ways of living and healing and growing.

Sarah Caldwell

All the time I was testing the universe, to see if it all really works, and it does. The results of my research I can not explain, I can only tell you and share with you what has worked for me and for others I have met.

Acknowledgments

To my children, my family and friends and others I have met along my life journey—they have made me who I am today. It really is true that people come into our lives for a reason.

I also want to acknowledge the many inspirational speakers and authors whose books, CDs and speeches have helped and taught me along the way. Thank you.

Introduction

In today fast paced life more and more people are turning to alternate healing and spiritualities. One form of healing and meditation that is becoming increasingly popular is crystals. We wear them on our bodies, we hold them in our hands, we put them under our pillow, and we display them in our homes. We use them to centre ourselves and heal our lives.

Why do so many of us choose to use crystals, is there really any benefit? Do they really work, why are they so popular, what is all the fuss about? Does meditating and talking to our angels and spirit guides really work? How and why, and does it work for everyone?

There are many instances throughout history and modern day life that show that using these 'alternate methods' of healing and meditation really work. Of course a positive 'I can do it' attitude helps, but even if we are sceptical, crystals, meditation, our guardian angels and spirit guides are going to help us, the trick is to believe and let them in to help us heal. When we change our way of thinking, be open to all the possibilities of the universe and miracles can happen.

This book aims to give a quick overview of some history and the why and how this healing works, and provide some practical ways to bring this healing and wisdom into our lives. It covers crystals and crystal healing, meditation and a little about how our angels and guides can help us.

1. Frequently Asked Questions

Why crystals?

Do people really use crystals for healing and meditation or is it just a gimmick? Do people really choose crystal jewellery and decoration for their healing properties? And if they do, why isn't the use of crystals more widely written about and talked about? Why isn't it in all the popular media? Is it a secret for only hippies and witches?

For any of us who use crystals for healing and meditation, while we may be hippies and / or witches we choose to use them because they work. Yes crystals look pretty and feel nice and enhance the beauty of our home. They also have their own unique vibration that helps and heals our lives in so many ways.

Why don't we hear more about this? Well maybe it's because we are scared that we will be called a hippie or a witch or that people won't believe us or think we are strange. Maybe it's because it could be awfully hard to prove a claim that crystals healed our illness or found us our soul mate or our dream house or dream job. Maybe it's because it's enough for us that crystals work for us, and while we may be happy to share this knowledge with some people we are uncomfortable with shouting it from the roof tops!

Some people's belief and lifestyle is such that their whole house and spirit is about crystal. They live and breathe crystals and meditations and are not afraid what other people think. Some people try using crystals and when they work they are quietly confident, or sceptical, depending on many circumstances. Then there are others who try these alternate forms of healing and decide to change aspects of their lives once they realise it works. What we do with the wisdom given to us is up to us.

Why are people attracted to crystals?

Is it just because of their interesting shapes and textures, the various colours or is there something else?

Crystals are pretty and interesting and for some people it's enough that they are aesthetically pleasing to the eye, either worn as jewellery or in displays around the home, and they don't think twice about any possible healing powers. More and more people are learning that crystals have healing powers and are willing to try using them in meditation or to heal aspects of their lives. Crystals have been used for healing and protection for thousands of years, some of this history is described in more detail later in this book. It has been scientifically proven that crystals emit a vibration and an energy of their own. This energy can heal all sorts of ailments, from mental to physical dis-ease, creating an aura of good luck or positivity in and around the home and in and around the person who uses, holds or works with crystals.

What do crystals do?

How can they have healing powers?

Crystals, formed from deep beneath the earth, have an energy of their own. Although most of us can not see, feel or hear the vibration that a crystal gives off, it is this energy or vibration that aide our well being. Some people are particularly sensitive to a crystals vibration and can feel this, but even if we can't feel this energy, it is still healing us. Each type of crystal—rose quartz, amethyst etc are formed with a particular molecular structure and it is from that that the vibration and energy flows.

When we take the time to sit and hold our crystals, thinking, or meditating or just gazing at our crystals, they work to heal all sorts of illnesses, or dis-ease. Even when we don't sit holding or staring at our crystals, the aura (energy) from the crystal is still helping to heal and aide our mental and physical wellbeing. The aura of good luck, the positive and wellness imbued in the crystal is always there even when we don't see, hear or feel it. Wherever the crystal is, it is sending out its own special energy to enhance our lives.

In very simple terms, if we have crystals around the house, and we like them and smile when we see them, if we touch them and it makes us feel happy or at peace, then they are working.

How do I make crystals work?

What do I do with them?

Do they have to touch my skin?

To "make crystals work" simply spend time with them each day (five minutes every day is enough), holding them, thinking positive thoughts about how you want your life to be, meditating, asking for guidance. Of course we can spend longer than five minutes each day if we want to. At the end of this book are some meditations to use for specific healing and day to day issues we need help with. No matter what it is we want in our lives, we can use crystals. Ask the crystals to help bring what it is you want from life, ask them for guidance and wisdom and insight and be amazed at the results.

Even if / when you don't have time to meditate, hold the crystal in your hand, stick it in your pocket, your handbag, (or your bra), in your car, under your pillow, or on your desk or somewhere in your workplace. The crystal is always working, not just when we ask it to. The crystals don't have to touch our skin to heal, though some people believe the healing energy is enhanced if the crystals are touching our skin.

Historically some healers and people who used crystals for all sorts of healing purposes would make a crystal essence to be taken internally by either crushing the crystals into a power form or by putting the crystals in mineral water. It's up to us to use our crystals in a way that works for us.

There are many ways and places to use you crystals. They can be placed around the home, at you work place and on yourself or others. They can be used in pendulums and for scrying. You can use them to cleanse your environment, for protection, creating types of energy or mood, for healing and relaxation, to assist meditation, to attract or repel, and anything else your imagination can conceive.

Can I hold other peoples crystals?

It has often been said that crystals choose a person and that you can not touch another persons crystals.

While it is true that by some spiritual, vibrational sign, energy or signal unknown to us, we do choose the crystal we are meant to have, there is absolutely no reason why we can't touch another person's crystal. If you are particularly concerned about someone else touching your crystals there are some simple ways your crystals can be cleansed. After all, throughout their journey, crystals come in contact with many people and substances yet always maintain the same energy and vibrance.

Do I have to clean them and how?

Why do we cleanse crystals?

By their very properties and by virtue of their unique vibrational energy, crystals are 'self cleansing' and so don't have to be cleaned. Some people feel that because our crystals come to us from so far away, that cleansing them makes them our own.

On their journey to us, crystals first are taken from the earth and then they are broken and cut into pieces. Some are tumbled and polished and others left in clusters or rough pieces. They are transported around the world to wholesalers and retail shops. In the shops they are handled by staff and many customers before they find their new home with us.

On their journey, the crystals will come into contact with the energy of each person who handles them. We can cleanse crystals to remove any unwanted energies they have collected, so they can become part of us. We can clean our crystals by:

- Washing them in salt water;

- Washing them under running water;
- Sitting them out to catch some sunlight;
- Burying them in the earth;
- Putting them out in a full moon;
- using Reiki or white light energy; or
- smudging with incense or a herbal smudge stick.

Leaving our crystals out in the full moon also assists in re-charging or boosting their healing properties.

To program our crystals for a specific purpose, healing for example— pick up the crystal and think about what you want it to do as you use it. Sit quietly holding your crystal and focus you mind on receiving help from the universe. Allow your body to receive the desired energy form the universe. Visualise this energy entering your crystal.

Does meditation really work?

Taking time out from everyday stresses and busyness has got to be of benefit. Taking time for ourselves, whether it is for five minutes each day, or for hours helps calm and relax us, creating peace and harmony in and around us and our lives. Try it—take a couple of minutes, right now where you are and close your eyes. Imagine are in your favourite spot, smiling, surrounded by people or things you love. Okay so when you opened your eyes, how did you feel? Less stressed? Happy? A little calmer? The results speak for themselves, the trick is to take the time to meditate.

How do I meditate? I don't have a lot of time—how long will it take?

Do I have to lie down?

While the idea of sitting, relaxing and dreaming for hours on end may seem appealing, not many of us have that luxury. Five minutes or more each day is all it takes. Meditation has a multiplier effect, the more you practice the greater the benefit. Don't worry if your mind wanders while you are meditating. It is normal for everyday thought and issues to pop up while you are being still and quiet. Simply bring your mind back to the thought or intention you started with, or look at your candle, crystals whatever you are using to focus and calm your mind again.

While you need to be comfortable to meditate, you don't specifically need to sit or lie in a certain way—as long as you are comfortable, relaxed and if possible uninterrupted. If it is at all possible take the phone off the hook, move into a room away from others, telling them that you don't want to be disturbed for a certain amount of time. You can sit (or lie) in any position that suits you. There are some meditations later on in the book to guide you as you start to meditate.

Where and when is the best time to meditate?

Some people find meditating first thing in the morning is great and sets a positive tone for the day. Others find it better to meditate after work as a way of winding down and relaxing. We may find ourselves falling asleep, especially if we meditate lying down after work, as we quickly become relaxed and peaceful. Short answer again is—whatever suits you and fits in with your lifestyle—morning, afternoon, evening, in the car, at home, at work, lying down or sitting—it has to work for you. Meditation has to be something you want to do and look forward to doing, not a chore you have to do.

Do I need anything special?

No, however you can use a candle, crystals, a photograph or other item to help you focus and centre yourself.

How do I talk to my angels and spirit guides? Who are my angels and spirit guides? How do I know they are there?

We all have one guardian angel, who is with us from when we are born, throughout our whole lives until we return to heaven. We all have many other angels and spirit guides around us at different times in our lives. Whether or not we believe in our angels and guides, whether or not we think they can help us they are there, wanting to help and guide us.

Talking to our angels and spirit guides is easy. Imagine someone who loves you unconditionally and wants the very best for you. What would you say to that person? You can think the thoughts, speak them out loud, or write down your thoughts and feelings. Some people think in images when communicating with their angels and guides. Again the answer is, whatever you feel comfortable with is the best way to have a conversation with your angels and guides.

What can they help with and how?

Your angels and guides want you to be happy and at peace. They can guide your thoughts—that intuition we feel in many situations—the one we so often ignore—that's our angels and guides trying to show us the way to achieve what it is we want from our lives. We may hear a certain song, smell a particular smell, see a feather or a butterfly or something else that means something to us—that's our angels and guides communicating with us. We may find seeming random thoughts or ideas popping into our mind—that's our angels, we may repeatedly see certain colours, or foods, or cars, or numbers, or other image—that's our angels. They will try to get their message across any way they can. Lucky for us they are patient and loving with us, even when we seem to ignore them.

2. History

Crystals

Ever since the earliest civilisations have passed down and eventually written their stories, the use of crystals for healing has been documented, dating back as far as humankind, as far as there are records of history. Ancient cultures and civilizations have used crystals in medicine and health care, for protection, magic and rituals, as offerings and currency, scrying or gazing for divination, for good luck and wealth as well as precious gifts and items of beauty. They were used to make elixirs and as a "first aid" tool. Archaeologists have discovered evidence of the prehistoric use of crystals in Europe, the Middle East, Russia and Africa. They found jewellery and carvings of amber, jet, turquoise, lapis, garnet, carnelian, quartz, and other stones. It is believed that the carvings were amulets and talismans. They found stones carved in the shape of animals, symbols of totems. The value given to crystals in these various cultures is indicated by their presence in the graves; they were intended to go with the departed soul to help them in the next life.

Crystal was widely used in Ancient Egypt. Hieroglyphics fom the year 2000 B.C. documents a medical cure using a crystal, as do several from the year 1500 B.C. Lapis Lazuli was considered to be a royal stone, often pulverized and made into a poultice to be rubbed into the crown of the head. It was believed that as it dried it drew out all spiritual impurities. The pharaohs often had their headdresses lined with malachite in the belief that it helped them to rule wisely. In powder form this stone was used for poor eyesight and inner vision. Other stones found in the tombs, include carnelian, turquoise, and tiger's eye. These were often shaped into amulets, shields, and into the shapes of hearts.

The Native Americans of North, Central, and South America used crystals widely for spiritual, ceremonial, and healing purposes. Obsidian was used by the Mayans for ceremonial knives; other tribes believed that it served to sharpen both outer and inner vision. Turquoise was believed to be a stone which bridged heaven and earth. Mayan Indians used quartz crystals for both the diagnosis and treatment of disease.

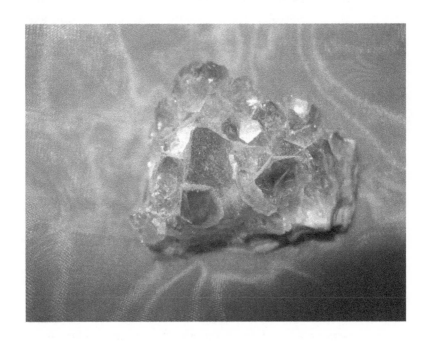

Quartz was traditionally revered in the Asia /Far East, especially in carved form. Quartz crystal balls were considered to represent the heart or essence of the dragons, thought to have great power and wisdom. The stone most associated with China is jade, the concentrated essence of love. Many kinds of amulets are carved from this stone, including those for friendship and for romantic love. A jade butterfly was a symbol of successful love.

The culture of ancient India is a rich source of information about crystals. The system of chakras (energy centres), a healing and meditation in which we place crystals on or around the body began there. Astrological documents written as early as 400 B.C. contain details about the power of various stones to counteract the negative effects of planetary positions. Stones were regarded as having great spiritual and emotional powers. Moonstone, for instance, was a sacred stone, and believed to arouse love. Onyx, in contrast, was believed to help release the ties of old loves. The ruby was a highly valued gemstone, and was known as the "king of precious stones."

The bible makes mention of crystals over 200 times, an example in Exodus, where the High Priest, Aaron, (brother of Moses) was instructed by God to make breast plate from particular crystals which he was to wear for protection and wisdom.

History has shown that:

- crystals and stones have a subtle effect on our bodies— when worn close to us their energy systems assist to bring about healing;
- the practice of taking gemstone powderers internally can heal, as can placing gemstone powders on our bodies;
- there are scientific explanations behind crystals healing 'powers'—the key to this is in the vibrations, of both the crystals and our bodies;
- It has been proven that the human mind can indeed interact with the crystal to create effects on the body,

mind and spirit, while Science can not currently explain how crystals can play a part in healing. The combination of perfect form and energy are the processes through which crystals encourage our bodies to come into balance and why they are such powerful tools for self-healing.

- Crystal healers use stones formed by nature in order to enjoy a tangible connections with the Earth and to tap into the energies of the mineral kingdom.

The word crystal comes from a Greek word Crystallos, from "Krysos" meaning "ice cold." Crystals come from the period in history when the earth was forming, the heating and cooling of the earth forming the magnificent crystals we have today. Most crystals are formed from silicon and oxygen which when they combine, form silicon dioxide, otherwise known as quartz. The other elements which are present during this combining of elements are what create the different types of crystals and contribute to its properties.

When a crystal is shattered, each piece may vary in size, but the fragments all have the same shape. The outer crystal reflects a larger version of the inner structure, consisting of one of several basic shapes.

Meditation

The history of meditation goes back many thousands of years. Yoga meditation techniques were received from the gods by the wise men of India as a way to a path to self salvation, allowing us a way back into union with our divine creator spirit.

These teachings were initially passed on by word of mouth from one wise Priest to another in the form of chants, or mantras. These poems or verses were later written down, forming part of the most ancient text on earth called the Mahabharata.

Archaeologists can date Yoga and meditation back to 3000 BC, so it appears that Yoga and meditation have been used for at least 5000 years.

There is not a lot written about the beginning of other forms of meditation, although its origins can be traced back to ancient times. Researchers think primitive hunter-gatherer societies may have discovered meditation and its altered states of consciousness while staring at the flames of their fires. Over thousands of years, meditation evolved into a more structured practice. Indian scriptures mention meditation techniques 5000 years ago.

Buddha's teachings spread far and wide across the Asian continent, and other countries and cultures adopted different forms of the word "meditation," and created their own unique way of practicing it. Buddhist style meditation practices are still popular today, spreading across to Western society thousands of years after it was adopted in the East. It gained popularity in the West in the mid-20th century, and its increasing its popularity as more and more people are looking for a way to reconnect to peace, calmness and happiness in our crazy fast paced society.

Angels and Spirit Guides

Everyone has a guardian angel, whether or not we believe in them or not, whether we listen to them or not, talk to them or not, they are there. Our guardian angel stays with us from birth until we return to heaven. Our angels love for us is unconditional and bigger than anything on this earth. Our guardian angel makes sure we are safe, protected and guided on our journey.

Guardian angels are sometimes confused with "spirit guides." A spirit guide is a loving being who has lived upon the earth in human form. Most spirit guides are deceased loved ones, such as grandparents, siblings, beloved friends, and parents. This person then received special training in the afterlife about how to become a spirit guide. Many of us have many angels and spirit guides around us throughout our lives.

Your spirit guide may have passed-away in the physical life before you were born. However, this loving being was there at your birth and has been with you every day of your life since. Just as you will always take an interest in your family's future offspring, so do the deceased family members whom we may have never encountered in physical form.

Our angels and guides do not interfere with our free will or make decisions for us. They are near us to give us general advice, comfort, and at times warning and protection. Our spirit guides act in the capacity of guardian angels, in that they bring many gifts to our lives. The main difference is that true guardian angels, who have never walked as mortals upon the earth, have a higher vibrating energy frequency. People who are empathic, who can "feel" the sensation of a spiritual presence, can tell the palpable difference between an angelic and a spirit guide appearance. Clairvoyants see that angels' aura is bright white, whereas a spirit guide's aura is not quite as bright and may appear as a bluish-white. We may sense or feel there is someone around us, maybe we sometimes catch a glimpse of them out of the corner of our eye.

Know that our guides and angels are always there should we need their knowledge or protection, or if we just want to say hello.

3. A true story

When we feel like things are not going right or when we are not achieving what we want to, it's because our body or our mind is out of balance. We might want something good to happen—find true love, a great job, a beautiful home,—but deep down we think we don't deserve what it is we want. While we think that it won't happen to us, then it won't happen to us, or at least it will take much longer to achieve our goal.

The good news is, by changing the way we think, by spending time thinking about and meditating about what it is was want, we can change how our life is going. It's not as hard as it sounds; there is no secret or magic formula that we have to know before we can succeed. All we have to do is spend time thinking about all the good things that we want in our lives, and believe that we can have all that we want. Imagine we have already achieved what it is we want. The key is to change the way we think so that we are positive in our beliefs. The more often we can catch ourselves when we start to be negative and turn our thoughts into positives, the more quickly we will see positive changes in our lives.

When we think about what we want, picture our lives as if we have already achieved our goal. Dream about the future as if it is a reality now, feel the happiness, the joy, the peace and the love of being exactly where we want to be.

We don't have to make any huge life changing decision; all we have to do is take five minutes each day. Whether we want to find the love of our life, our soul mate, more money, travel, health, happiness, career or our dream house, we only need to find five minutes quiet time each day. Of course we can spend more time with our crystals if we want to. The catch is, we have to persevere and stick at it, taking the time each day to spend in contemplation and meditation, and not give up if we don't see results immediately.

We are retraining ourselves to think positively while at the same time allowing the crystals to heal and bring us what we are asking for.

I used to be sceptical, thinking that all that was written about this type of healing and achieving worked for others and not me. I used to think it was a waste of time, that no amount of dreaming or visualising would make what I want happen. Then three events changed my life and my way of thinking.

Firstly I was diagnosed with cancer, in the form of a growing lump in my leg. It didn't look good. The doctors were using words such as 'aggressive' and 'spread through the body'. Although I knew the lump was cancer and had suspected this far before the doctors' diagnosis, I refused to give up. I have four beautiful children and I refused to believe that the universe would do this to me, I could not believe that I would not be there for them as they grew up. I read all I could about healing. I used meditation, visualisation, crystals and colour healing and imagined the bright, white, healing light blasting away the cancer and healing my body. I imagined seeing my children as teenagers, growing up. I imagined being a part of their lives. I was terrified, but I persisted with the visualisations and the white light healing. Through the weeks of tests to see how far the cancer had spread I kept up the visualisation, as many times a day as I could. I pictured seeing my kids grow up, seeing them ten years older than they were. I meditated on flying through the rainbow of colours, letting the green heal me, the pink spread peace throughout my body and the white healing light spreading through my body, the cancer being blasted away and disappearing. A couple of weeks later, all the tests came back clear. The doctors, after more investigation discovered that the lump was no longer cancer.

My life changed for the better and I continued to use this technique. There was a house I wanted to buy but I didn't have the money I needed to buy it. I didn't know how I was going to get the house, but each night I visualised myself in the house, cooking, entertaining and living in it. Despite many potential buyers, the house didn't sell. The house was perfect for me and my family it was our house. I knew it and so did the house. There were enough bedrooms for all of us, enough space and a great garden and backyard. Then one day I realised that the kids were only going to be with me for a couple of more years and then I would be in the huge house by myself. I let go of the house and within the week it sold. I have no doubt that it only sold when I decided that my life path did not include that house.

I decided to use the same technique for finding my soul mate. At the same time as I was visualising my house I was using the same visualisations for my job and I was successful with winning my job. I figured that I had nothing to lose, as any relationship I had been in had been with people who I really didn't like. Previously I had decided that the only people who would be interested in me would be the average bloke, not too smart, someone who needed me as I was smarter and more successful than them. I guess that it should have been no surprise that the only people I had been out with were lame ducks, dumb as mud, guys who fitted that exact description.

What I really wanted in my soul mate was someone I could talk to about anything. Not necessarily deep and meaningful conversations, but just talk. Like my best friends in high school and at university. These guys I could talk to about anything, intelligent conversation. I wanted someone intelligent, challenging, clever, who loved fun, someone I could connect with on every level. I began to imagine myself with this person, someone who was just like my best mates at high school and university.

Around the same time I spent Christmas at the beach, by myself. My children were with their father and his family, and although I had plenty of invitations for lunch and dinners with friends, I opted for the soothing, healing peaceful strength of the ocean. In the cabin I rented I set up my candles, my crystals, my angel cards and other symbols I collected. I went for long walks, meditating and collecting symbols. There was a shell, a leaf, a stone and a stick. During my time at the beach thoughts and ideas of the type of person, and words and a melody, a song kept going around and around in my head about the person I was going to be with.

Not five months later a chance encounter at work and several seemingly isolated incidents led me to meet my partner. He is smart, clever, intelligent funny, and quite a challenge! We met and became friends first and the relationship grew. It was painfully, frustratingly slow and still is to some extent, we are both cautious as we have both been hurt before. But he is amazing, exactly who I visualised. We don't live together but spend a lot of time together, as a couple and with our children. There are ups and downs in our relationship, but there is meant to be, it's through life that we learn and grow. I am now working on visualising us living together, and although we aren't yet, I know that we will in the future, when the time is right. The funny thing is, if we had met years ago, we wouldn't be the same people and wouldn't be in the wonderful relationship we are in now.

So that's my story, to date anyway.

Not that I am saying that I have everything I want, but I now know the secret to having what it is I want in my life.

Its about more than just having the crystals,—though that's a very good start. We need to spend time with our crystals, in meditation and contemplation, imagining what it is we want, believing it already exists in our life, living as if we have already got it. This is the bit I sometimes find hard to stick to. Sure I have crystals in my house, my car, under my pillow, in my handbag, on my desk and on some days in my clothes, but I still have times of doubt. I still have days when I don't believe I will ever get everything I truly desire. And you know the truth about the universe giving us what we ask for and think about, so if I am thinking that I wont get my house, my dream job or the love of my life, the universe will oblige, and it will take longer to achieve my aim.

The other catch is, if we are not sure what it is we really want, it will take longer for the universe to deliver, as it cant understand our indecision and so can not deliver what it is if we don't know what it is we truly desire.

So what we need to do (and it doesn't take a lot of time each day, the hardest part into getting into a routine with our crystals) is to spend some time each day sitting quietly, holding our crystals, and dreaming. Dream about the house we want, the family we want, the dream job, the holiday, the happy family, the amazing lover and partner, health, happiness, the answers to our questions—whatever it is our soul longs for. As I said before, imagine we are already right where we want to be. Be clear and positive and happy and be amazed at the results.

If we don't know what it is we truly want or we are confused or torn between situations, focus on and ask for answers to our questions, so that it will become clear to us what our focus should be, and where we want to be headed.

I use many different crystals throughout the day, and find candles, music and fragrances greatly enhance my ability to sit and meditate. The combination of all this together brings the wisdom from our angels and guides that much closer.

4. Holistic approach to healing

Crystals, crystal essences, colour healing, meditation, fragrances, chakras, angels, guides, candles and music—how do all these things help us heal? How does this all come together? What do we have to do to make this all happen, how quickly? And what if we forget part of it or do something wrong?

These things all work in harmony, its not like we have remember lots of different things, do lots of different things at different times, or spend hours in meditation and contemplation. If we have the best of intentions and don't want to hurt anyone, if we want the best for ourselves and everyone else, there is not really a way we can get it wrong. If we forget to be positive today or we are cranky tomorrow, but still want to create a wonderful healthy life, it will still work. Trust our intuition and listen to our angels and guides. Hold our crystals and ask for what we want. If we find ourselves being negative, acknowledge our feelings and turn it into a positive thought.

An example may be "My relationship with X isn't working, we will never be together" When we catch ourselves thinking this, stop and acknowledge—"Well that's how I used to think, but now I ask my guides to show me how to get over this problem and make our relationship better." If work is the problem and is getting us down, don't think negative thoughts about work, instead "I know that I can achieve great things at work, if only I listen to my intuition." Try it, it really works.

5. Daily use and guidance

How Crystals Work

It is a scientific fact that all matter is made up of energy, and that any object, a person, plant, a plastic pipe, grain of sand or body of water has energy within it and surrounding it., Energy resonates at a particular vibration, and for each object or thing, there is a specific vibration.

When we are 'functioning properly' each part of our body and even our emotions have their own specific vibrations. When the body or emotion is not healthy this vibration changes. Crystals can help "tune in" the vibration for the human body as well as for other living things such as plants and animals, as crystals always have the same vibration energy.

This is called the Theory of Resonance. Crystals are set in their formation, so unlike the human body, they do not alter in their vibration and "get sick" or out of balance. This makes them excellent for assisting the body and mind as the crystals stays constant in its vibration and will our body back into line with the crystal's "healthy" vibration.

Crystals have many uses:

- healing on a physical and emotional level;
- cleansing our environment;
- protection;
- relaxation;

- assisting with meditation;
- attracting things to us, e.g. love, money, luck, job, house, partner etc

The energy level that crystals work on is extremely subtle so don't be surprised if you feel nothing at first. As you work with crystals more and more, you will become attuned to their subtle, beautiful energy. Just being around them has a wonderful effect. Tuning in to the vibrational energy of crystals takes a little work. Some people are naturally quite sensitive to its energy and feel it the instant they come into contact with their first crystal, whilst for others it takes time and effort. The sensation of this energy is a similar feeling to Reiki energy, which works at the same level. Remember, don't be discouraged if you don't feel anything straight away. You can change the hand positions around to try to pick the energy up from different angles. Just keep practicing and you will eventually feel the energy in your hands. We are all different, so naturally we will 'tune-in' in our own time.

What do I do with my crystals?

As crystals either as tumblestones, raw rock clusters or other formations, in jewellery or essences have healing energy and vibrations, they can assist with many aspects of our lives. Some crystals compliment each other to help us to heal our bodies, our minds and other things we are struggling with. The list below gives some examples of the crystals and the type of healing they help with.

Although it is great to spend time each day in meditation and sitting quietly holding our crystals and focusing on our healing and improving our lives, we don't have to do this each day for the crystals to work. If we hold them somewhere on our body, keeping them close by as we go about our daily routine, we can occasionally touch them, hold them and think about our intention, sending our positive and healing thoughts out into the universe.

Where to put your crystals:

- on the table beside you;
- under your pillow;
- in your car;
- in your bra, handbag or pocket;
- at work on desk;
- in glass bowls as a decoration in our homes or workplace;
- In jewellery—touching your skin or not

6. Crystals and their uses

Love and family relationships

Rose Quartz—stone of unconditional love, healing and peace

Rhodonite—brings love and passion into action, clears and activates the heart chakra

Garnet—stone of love and attraction, inspires mutual attraction

Emerald—brings successful love, domestic bliss and security in love

Turquoise—stimulates romantic love and honesty

Agate—stone of protection and for clarity in important decisions

Amethyst—peace calmness and inspiration

Self Confidence

Onyx—brings self-confidence, the stone of self-control

Hematite—strengthens self-esteem and self-confidence

Sunstone—promotes self-worth, enthusiasm and optimism

Amazonite—brings confidence, allows heartfelt expression

Iolite—stimulates inner strength and confidence

Depression

Lapis Lazuli—stimulates personal power, relieves depression

Smokey Quartz—imparts a positive attitude, eases stress and depression

Rose Quartz—promotes self-worth, self-forgiveness and peace

Jet—eases depression and mood swings

Carnelian—attracts a love of life

Grounding

Hematite—provides grounding, concentration and focus

Jasper—stone of protection and grounding

Snowflake Obsidian—balances the mind and spirit, brings grounding

Bloodstone—grounding and protective, encourages adaptability

Onyx—provides self-mastery, a grounding stone

Good Luck and Money

Jade—brings good luck, wealth and self-sufficiency

Turquoise—provides good luck

Agate—fosters good luck and prosperity

Garnet—considered a good luck stone, repels negativity

Citrine—brings luck and wealth

Green Aventurine—brings luck and abundance

Stress / de Stress

Smokey Quartz—relieves stress, anxiety and depression, encourages calm

Moss Agate—lessens stress, instills tolerance

Agate—helps overcome stress, bitterness and inner agate

Amethyst—brings tolerance, peace and calmness, relieves stress

Aventurine—healer of the heart, mind and soul, relieves stress and brings a positive attitude

Tigers Eye—focuses the mind, clear thinking and insight

Clear Quartz—positive energy

Aquamarine—calming and quiets the mind

Grief

Onyx—banishes grief, promotes personal strength

Rose Quartz—soothes heartache and loss, promotes acceptance

Amazonite—dispels sadness, grief and negative energy

Jade—brings balance and healing

Tiger Eye—aids in dealing with difficult periods in one's life

Friendship

Tourmaline—promotes friendship, compassion, tolerance and caring

Emerald—instills sensitivity, truth and loyalty in self and others

Garnet—brings spirituality to friendships

Rhodonite—strengthens friendships and fosters humanity

Rose Quartz—stone of love and friendship, brings harmony and trust to relationships

Agate—Stone of protection, brings calm and inspiration

Memory

Howlite—strengthens memory

Emerald—aids memory and clarity

Hematite—enhances memory and problem solving, brings focus

Amethyst—allow one to clear and focus the mind, simulates memory

Sodalite—clears up mental confusion, fosters knowledge

Truth

Lapis Lazuli—stone of honesty, truthfulness and awareness

Agate—fosters honesty and harmony

Fluorite—helps one to see the truth and remain unbiased

Sodalite—encourages self-truthfulness

Obsidian—stone of truth and protection

Dreams

Clear quartz—positive stone enhances the energy in other crystals

Citrine—opens our mind to new thoughts

Jade—stone of good fortune

Amethyst—high mental clarity and insight

Lepidolite—promotes calmness and healing

Malachite—removes fear, encourages healthy relationships

Health / Healing

Jade—guards against accidents and misfortune

Rose Quartz—heals and brings peace and love

Tigers eye—protection stone, it clears and focuses our thoughts, bringing positive healing energy

Clear Quartz—this stone has powerful healing properties

Agate—Stone of protection, brings calm and inspiration

Amethyst—clears and focuses the mind

Amazonite—increases self respect, reduces self neglect

Carnelian—increases loving relationships

Aquamarine—calms mood swings and panic attacks

Moonstone—brings peace

Citrine—effective against depression and addiction

Other specific crystals(not listed here as the list would be huge) can assist in specific ailments

Happiness and Peace / House and Home

Rose Quartz—stone of love and friendship, brings harmony and trust to relationships

Clear Quartz—positive energy it brings love, peace and wisdom to any intention

Smoky Quartz—reduces anxiety and stress

Citrine—energises and restores health

Moss Agate—a crystal of new beginnings

Amethyst—brings peace, calmness and inspiration to our lives

Wisdom

Clear Quartz—stone of intuition, clarity and knowledge

Sodalite—stone of protection, brings calm and inspiration

Selenite—brings intuition, wisdom and knowledge

Lapis luzuli—responsibility for oneself and situations

Career

Red Tigers Eye—enthusiasm and optimism

Citrine—brings energy and clarity

Snoflake Obsinian—strengthens determination

Lapis Luzuli—responsibility and ownership of work and career

Imagination

Sodalite—brings calmness, peace and inspiration

Smoky Quartz—reducing anxiety and stress allows clarity and imagination to flow

Tigers Eye—works through grief and anger to provide answers and knowledge

Rhodochrosite—opens up physic and intuitive energy

Love and Soul Mate

Amethyst—brings peace, calmness and inspiration to our lives

Angelite—aids healing and communication in relationships

Aquamarine—attracts good luck and love and calms mood swings

Red Carnelian—heals jealousy and possessiveness

Rose Quartz—stone of love and friendship, brings harmony and trust to relationships

Communication

Blue Lapis Luzuli—assists with empowerment and speaking out

Moss agate—brings purpose and meaning, new beginnings

Turquoise—calms the mind and brings empowerment

Blue calcite—creates awareness of self and others

Travel

Adventurine—prevent against disruption and loss

Jade—protection from illness

Red Tigers Eye—protects against loss and theft

Malachite—protection and removes fear

Tree Agate—guards against fatigue

Courage

Jade—protection and brings good fortune

Sunstone—eases phobias

Blue Lace Agate—calms stress and communication problems

Black Onyx—empowerment and guards against addictions

Selenite—helps self identity

Sarah Caldwell

Protection

Blue Lace Agate—calms stress and communication problems

Amethyst—calms and reduces addictions and destructive behaviour

Turquoise—calms and protects

Sepentine—overcomes negative and harmful emotions

Snowflake Obsidian—strengthens determination and recovery after trauma

7. Meditations

Healing Meditation

Find a quiet place and light your candle, place your stones next to the candle

Take a deep breath in and release

Picture in your mind a bright white healing light surrounding you

Feel the light healing your body, dissolving illness and pain, you are once again healthy

Believe it has already happened

Do this at least once a day for a month

Happiness Meditation

Find a quiet place and light your candle, place your stones next to the candle

Take a deep breath in and release

Picture in your mind a bright white healing light surrounding you

Imagine travelling on your holiday, feel the sun shining down as you relax and have fun

Believe it has already happened Do this at least once a day for a month

Dream House Meditation

Find a quiet place and light your candle, place your stones next to the candle

Take a deep breath in and release

Picture in your mind a bright white healing light surrounding you

Imagine living in your dream house, with all the money you need to make it a beautiful place to live

Believe it has already happened

Do this at least once a day for a month

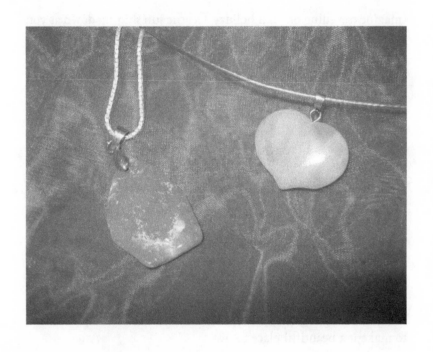

Dream Job Meditation

Find a quiet place and light your candle, place your stones next to the candle

Take a deep breath in and release

Picture in your mind a bright white healing light surrounding you

Let your mind focus on your dreams, imagine yourself in your dream job

Believe it has already happened

Do this at least once a day for a month

De Stress Meditation

Find a quiet place an light your candle, place your stones next to the candle

Take a deep breath in and release

Picture in your mind a bright white healing light surrounding you

Clear your mind of all your worries, the light is healing all your pain
Feel the calmness and peace all around you

Do this at least once a day for a month

Dreams Meditation

Find a quiet place and light your candle, place your stones next to the candle

Take a deep breath in and release

Picture in your mind a bright white healing light surrounding you

Let your mind focus on your dreams, imagine having what it is you want in your life

Believe it has already happened

Do this at least once a day for a month

Love Meditation

Find a quiet place and light your candle, place your stones next to the candle

Take a deep breath in and release

Picture in your mind a bright white healing light surrounding you

Let your mind focus on love, imagine and believe that you are already in a loving and wonderful relationship

Do this at least once a day for a month

Meditation with our angels

You can choose to communicate with your angels, by talking to them, thinking in images, pictures and by thinking about what you want to achieve with their help and guidance. Use candles, music and crystals if you want, but know they are always with us, ready to help.

Angels

These are the beings of light who respond to our calls for guidance, assistance, protection, and comfort. God's thoughts of love create angels. The angels are here to help us, especially when our intent is to bring joy and healing to the world. Ask for as many angels as you want to surround you. Ask for angels to surround your loved ones, your home, and your business. Angels receive great joy at helping us, and they ask only that we occasionally remember to say, "Thank you" in gratitude for their help.

Archangels

These are the angels who supervise the guardian angels and angels upon the earth. You might think of archangels as the "managers" among the earthly angels' hierarchy. You can call upon an archangel whenever you need powerful and immediate assistance.

Spirit Guides

Our Spirit Guides are entities or spirits who watches, teaches, heals, and helps us on our physical and spirit journey, throughout our life.

Communication is generally telepathic with words or images, stronger during meditation, dream time, or just by learning how to focus, look and listen to messages received. Some people call this method of connection channelling. The more you practice, the easier it gets.

We can call upon our angels and spirits guides to help us during all our meditations, healings and crystal work, just ask and they will be with us to help us. Mine have helped me share what I have learnt with you. I know they will help you with whatever you desire in your life.

8. Chakras

Chakra Healing

Our Chakras are our inner energy force, comprising of seven major energy centres and smaller energy centres that when they are all working well and in harmony assist our body and mind to function at its very best. Dis-ease, dis-harmony, pain, negative emotions and feelings, things that have happened in our past can all affect the balance in these energy centres, our Chakras. The good news is we can use crystals to get our chakras back into harmony and functioning properly. When we do this our body, mind and emotions are able to heal, and we will feel better, have more energy and achieve great things.

Starting from the base of our spine and working up towards the top of the head our chakras are associated with specific colours and crystals. Use any of the crystals listed below or a combination of the crystals when clearing and cleansing your chakras.

Chakra Meditation

This meditation can take five minutes or up to an hour, depending on the amount of time you want to focus on each crystal and chakra. You can choose the amount of time you take. You may want to put quiet music on to help you focus on your crystals. It is up to you.

1. If you like working with candles, light a candle near where you going to meditate, ask the candle to assist with your chakra healing.
2. Ask each of your crystals to help your chakras to clear and function at their very best.
3. Lie down placing the crystals near you, near your chakras, or place them on your body if you prefer.
4. Take a few deep breaths, letting the day's stresses and worries leave your body as you breathe out.
5. Starting with the Root Chakra and working up to the Crown Chakra—imagine each of the crystals energy entering your body and spreading through your body, healing any pain and hurt.
6. Feel the coloured light energy of each crystal as it moves through your body, feel its warmth and its healing energy.
7. Feel your body clearing itself of all pain and hurt as the healing light and energy works its magic.
8. When you are ready, slowly sit up, drink some water, and be amazed at the results.

Root (red)

Balanced: Physical power / strength
Unbalanced: Fear, anger, irritable
Red Jasper
Sardonyx
Serpentine
Jet
Snowflake Obsidian
Haematite
Tigers Eye

Sacral (orange)

Balanced: Sexual desire, pleasure, self esteem, balanced judgement and emotions
Unbalanced: Doubting self, scared of authority, stress
Snowflake Obsidian
Selenite
Yellow Calcite
Carnelian

Solar Plexis (yellow)

Integration of experiences, self-confidence, new opportunities
Workaholic, restless, indecisive, compulsive behavior
Citrine
Yellow Calcite
Snowflake Obsidian
Rhodochrosite
Tigers Eye

Heart (green and pink)

Balanced: compassion, self love, love of others
Unbalanced: emotional outbursts, possessive, jealous

Rose quartz
Green Adventurine
Malachite
Serpentine
Rhodonite
Rhodochrosite

Throat (light blue)

Balanced: clear communication, creativity, leadership qualities
Unbalanced: difficulty communicating, stutter, sarcasm, inappropriate language
Blue lace agate
Angelite
Sodalite

Third Eye (dark blue or purple)

Balanced: clairvoyant, imagination, healing, intuition
UnBalanced: headaches, inability to cope, not accepting life
Amethyst
Sodalite
Lapis Luzuli

Crown (violet, white or gold)

Balanced: integration of mind, body and spirit, wisdom, fulfilment of goals
Unbalanced: inability to value love, life and happiness, flu like symptoms
Clear quartz
Sepentine
Selenite

9. For further information

There are so many books, websites and people who can help us with our life journey, some of them are listed in the bibliography.

If you want any further information about anything specific you can email the author on

secaldwell@bigpond.com or
angelwisdom46@yahoo.com.au

Conclusion

We are in charge of our own life journey and our own healing.

We can choose an "I Can Do It" attitude and get on with the joy of living.

The universe, our Guardian Angels, Angels and Spirit Guides are there to help and guide us.

Crystals have their own vibrational energy that we can use to heal our body, mind, spirit, emotions and to create a life full of love and joy.

It is easy to talk to our angels and spirit guides.

Meditation can take as little as five minutes a day.

We can all choose happiness, love, life and abundance and we don't have to do it alone.

About the author

Sarah Caldwell

Author of children's stories, meditations and a single parent guide, Sarah is a single parent to four beautiful children. Sarah is also an Angel Card Reader, a Reiki Therapy Healer, a childcare worker, teacher, author and motivational speaker.

Born and raised in a country town, currently living in 'the big city' Sarah is still not sure where she wants to live when she grows up, but knows she wants to live near a beach.

When diagnosed with cancer a few years ago Sarah used the power of visualisation, meditation, her angel guides and crystals healing energy to counteract the disease—she wasn't ready to leave her family and has used these techniques ever since. Knowing how much better she feels when she takes time out to meditate and how well she doesn't feel when she doesn't she wants to share this reality with everyone.

Her range of crystal meditation healing bags, jewellery and candles further enhances her work and she is available for crystal party plan evenings, speaking engagements, and in addition to her standard healing kits, she takes orders for special healing bags.

Light heartedly accused of being a hippie and a witch by her nearest and dearest, she wants to share what she has learnt with everyone and also is available for Reiki healing and Angel card readings. She is willing to travel anywhere in Australia to help others.

Resources

The author, Sarah has a range of crystal meditations kits, jewellery and candles available for purchase at a discounted price to readers of this book. Sarah will make up your own personalised healing meditation kit if you send her an email explaining what it is you would like.

Bibliography

Websites:

A to Z index of crystals, their meanings and their role in history

http://www.gemstonegifts.com/resources/healing.htm

http://www.crystalinks.com/gemstones.html

http://www.rainbowcrystal.com/crystal/newage.html

http://www.crystalage.com/crystal_information/crystal_history/

Books:

Eason, Cassandra. (2010) *The New Crystal Bible*. Cameron House / Australia

Hall, Judy. (2010) *The Crystal Bible*. Godsfield Press / Hamlyn

Hay, Louise L. (1991) *You Can Heal Your Life*. Hay House

Hay, Louise L and Richardson, Cheryl. (2011) *You Can Create an Exceptional Life*. Hay House

Holden, Robert. (2011) *Shift Happens* Hay House